Fun with Computer Electronics

by Luann Colombo

Illustrations by Peter Georgeson

Andrews and McMeel
A Universal Press Syndicate Company
Kansas City

Dedication

Conn McQuinn's wit and wisdom reign supreme in his CD-ROM Fun with Computer Electronics. *He and his works have once again been my driving force and true inspiration.*

Special thanks to Hugh (Bounce) Vartanian, my electronics consultant, who helped me "chip" away at this book. Thanks for the Sparks!

The *Fun with Computer Electronics* packaged set is produced by becker&mayer!, Ltd.

Fun with Computer Electronics copyright © 1996 by Luann Colombo. Illustrations © 1996 by Peter Georgeson. All rights reserved. Printed in Canada. No part of this book may be used or reproduced in any manner whatsoever without written permission except in the case of reprints in the context of reviews. For information, write Andrews and McMeel, a Universal Press Syndicate Company, 4520 Main Street, Kansas City, Missouri 64111.

From the *Fun with Computer Electronics* packaged set, which includes electronic parts, an electronic workbench, wires, and this book.

Electronic circuit design: Jim Becker, Jim Snell, and Steve Monsey

Package and book design: Susan Hernday

ISBN: 0-8362-2306-3

Contents

Introduction

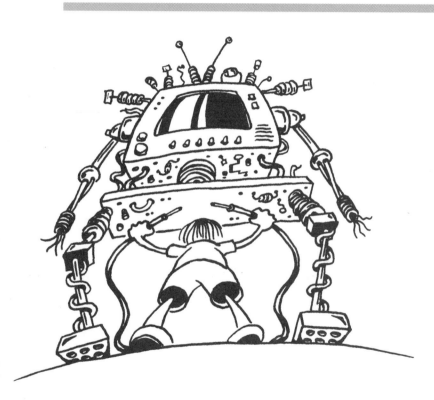

Welcome to *Fun with Computer Electronics*!

Computers! They're everywhere! But just what do they do? And, more importantly, how do they do it? With this book and kit you will use computer chips and many other components that are found in real computers to discover how computers work. You will build and experiment with 20 different really cool digital projects. How about making a Siren with Flashing Lights, a Reaction Timer, even a Digital Dice game? Sound like fun? Well, it is!

This book will also answer some of those burning questions like: What is electricity? What's a chip? How does a computer think?

Before you can perfect your digital wizardry, you must first assemble your electronic workbench. (Even Edison had to have a workshop.) Your kit comes with a gazillion parts—springs, wires, chips, and other electronic components found in your toolbox. Components are what scientists and technicians call the little electronic pieces. (When you don't know what to call something with a wire on it, call it a component and you'll be cool.) Once you follow the instructions VERY carefully, you will be ready to build 20 mind-boggling and friend-dazzling projects. Good luck!

What Is Electricity?

Before we can even get to the mystery of how a computer works, we first have to discuss the mystery of how electricity works. Electricity is the invisible fuel that runs the computer. In fact, electricity is the power that runs lots of things in our lives. Look around you. I bet there are at least 10 things in your workroom that are powered by electricity. Count them: lights, clocks, computer, TV, radio, the door (OK, probably not the door but you get the point). Electricity is EVERYWHERE! But if we can't see it, how do we know it's there?

It all starts with "atoms"—the tiny, invisible building blocks that make up everything. Atoms have even tinier parts, called "electrons" that circle around them. These electrons each have a teeny, tiny electric charge and are so small that a hundred million of them lined up wouldn't make it across the period at the end of this sentence.

Electrons like to circulate around their own atoms, but there are times when they get thrown from one atom to another. When lots of atoms pass along lots of electrons in the same direction, it's called ELECTRICITY, or an "electrical current."

The electrons move when there are too many of them in one place. You can't see this happen, but you can sure feel it—for example, when you get shocked by someone who has scuffed his or her feet on a carpet. (Ouch! I really hate it when that happens.)

Insulators and conductors

The Stop and Go of Electric Flow

Materials that electricity can flow through are called "conductors." Many metals, such as copper, aluminum, and iron, are great conductors of electricity.

Plastic, rubber, and glass are poor conductors. They are called "electrical insulators," which is why plastic and rubber are often used to cover conductors such as metal wires. This way, if you touch an insulated wire, the electricity won't shock you.

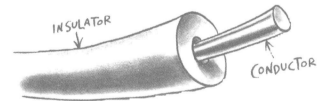

In your kit, the metal wire is the conductor and the colored plastic coating on the wire is the insulator.

How electricity moves

Electrons can't go anywhere if there isn't something pulling or pushing them. The usual reason for electrons to move is when there is an imbalance—too many electrons in one place, and not enough in another. Then the electrons will move around to even out things.

In your circuit board, the battery supplies this imbalance. The positive terminal has an electron deficit (few), and the negative terminal has an electron surplus (many). When the battery is hooked up, the electrons flow from the negative terminal through the wires and circuits to the positive terminal.

One of the ways electricity is measured is "voltage." Your battery for this kit is a nine-volt battery.

All this electricity flow can only work when there is a complete loop all the way from the negative to the positive terminal on the battery. This is called a "complete circuit." If one of the wires gets disconnected, the atoms can't keep passing along their electrons, and the electrons—and the electricity—come to a screeching halt.

Computer Basics

What is a "chip"?

"Well, it's chocolate and is found in America's favorite cookies."

"No! Not that kind of chip. A computer chip!"

"Oh."

Chips are where the computer stores and processes information. The fancy name for them is "integrated circuit." Each chip is made of a material called silicon. It's also the main ingredient in beach sand. Specially treated silicon is a "semiconductor," which means that sometimes it will conduct electricity, and sometimes it won't. This property is used to create microscopic transistors, which act as tiny electronic on-and-off switches.

On the surface of the chip are lots of miniature transistors. There can be hundreds, or even millions, of transistors on a chip.

9

To grow a chip

To create a chip, first you must grow purified silicon into long, sausage-shaped crystals. These crystals are cut into thin slices called "wafers." Transistors are created on the wafers in a long, complicated process. Each completed wafer holds dozens of individual chips.

The chips are mounted into housings with metal legs. This protects them and makes them easy to install into circuit boards. These are the kinds of chips you'll be using in your projects. Go look at one of your chips. Doesn't it look like a centipede from outer space?

What do chips do?

In a computer, some chips simply store information—they're called "memory chips." Some chips have special purposes, like translating computer data into sound, or video pictures, or controlling the disk drive. There are thousands of different special-purpose chips.

In a computer, though, the most important chip is the microprocessor. This chip handles virtually all of the computer program instructions that make everything else go. It controls all the major functions of the computer, including where information is stored, what you see on the screen, how to work math computations, even when to beep.

The microprocessor chip is the most complicated and expensive chip in the computer. A modern microprocessor chip has as many as 6 million transistors squeezed onto a space that is less than an inch across. Under a microscope it looks like the street map of a large city.

How do computers think?

A computer can't second-guess what you're trying to tell it. Computers handle information in very simple terms. Everything they do is broken down into questions that can be answered "yes" or "no." Information that goes into computers is called "input." Information that comes out of computers is called "output" (how clever). Computers work these questions with special decision makers called "gates." These gates look at two different incoming pieces of information, both of which are either "yes" or "no," and send out one new piece of information, also either "yes" or "no." Different gates respond to the input in different ways. These gates have names like AND, NAND, OR, and XOR. You'll be making each of these gates on your digital workbench.

How Do Computers Work?

I bet you've used a computer—or at least seen one, or you wouldn't have been interested in this book in the first place. Many computers were used to produce this book and electronic workbench. But let's look inside to see how they work.

The **MONITOR** is the OUTPUT for the computer. The CPU sends information to the screen so you can tell what the computer is doing.

RAM (Random-Access Memory) is a memory chip that you can read and that you can write on—like a notebook. It's temporary storage. Information in RAM is lost when the power is turned off.

CPU (Central Processing Unit) is the brains of the computer and performs all the arithmetic and logic functions. The CPU consists of many electronic circuits on a single microprocessor chip. It gets information from input and from memory.

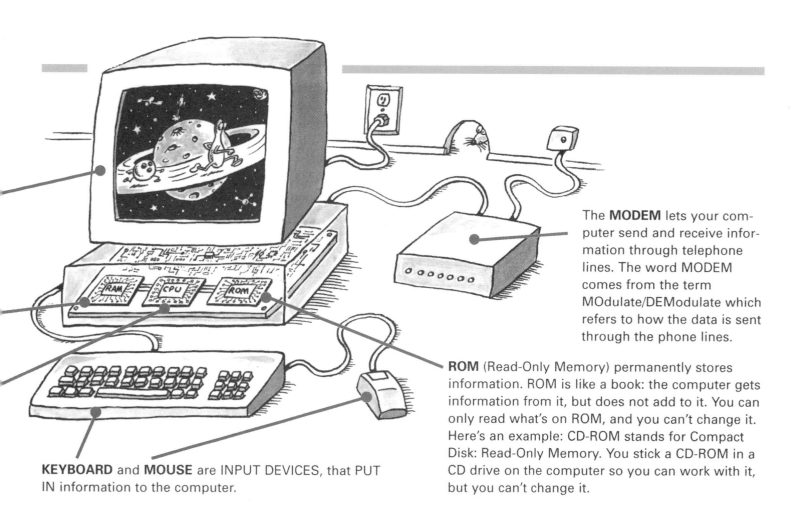

The **MODEM** lets your computer send and receive information through telephone lines. The word MODEM comes from the term MOdulate/DEModulate which refers to how the data is sent through the phone lines.

ROM (Read-Only Memory) permanently stores information. ROM is like a book: the computer gets information from it, but does not add to it. You can only read what's on ROM, and you can't change it. Here's an example: CD-ROM stands for Compact Disk: Read-Only Memory. You stick a CD-ROM in a CD drive on the computer so you can work with it, but you can't change it.

KEYBOARD and **MOUSE** are INPUT DEVICES, that PUT IN information to the computer.

Assembly Instructions

It's time to assemble your electronic workbench! (Engineers call this a "bread board"—but I wouldn't eat off of it.) Once you've put this together, you'll be ready to build many way cool digital circuits.

First, open up the cardboard workbench, and punch out the two pre-cut pieces on the back side of the workbench labeled "Binary Numbers" and "Digital Dice." Save these pieces—you'll use them for some of the projects you're going to build later.

Next, open the plastic box containing the electrical components. Take the small springs and insert them into the round holes next to the numbers on the project board. Put them in small end first, about halfway. It might look like a lot—68 to be exact—but trust me, you're gonna need

them. If the holes aren't punched all the way through, simply take a pen or pencil and push the extra cardboard through the hole before inserting the spring.

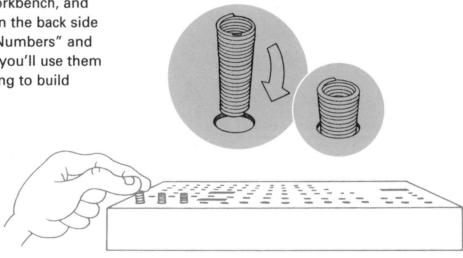

Part One

Light Emitting Diodes

Light Time

The next step is to install the Light Emitting Diodes, or "LEDs" for short. They're the red plastic cans with two wires sticking out. Diodes are one-way valves for electricity, and are the simplest of the electronic parts called semiconductors. As you already know, conductors let electrons flow easily, and insulators don't let them flow at all. So a semiconductor is halfway between. It is a conductor when electricity is flowing in the right direction, and an insulator when electricity is flowing in the wrong direction.

LEDs are special diodes because they give off light when electricity passes through them. Of course, because they are diodes they only let electricity flow in one direction.

Hold up one of your LEDs to the light. That metal you see inside is called a "semiconductor junction." It's kind of a big word for such a small part, but this is the part that allows electrical current to flow in only one direction. LEDs are used on computers, stereos, TVs, video games, calculator numbers, alarm clocks, VCRs, and many other electronic gizmos. On your project board they are being used to guide you to digital enlightenment.

In your kit you have 10 LEDs which get installed like this: Put the legs of the LED's through the small holes between the springs marked 1 and 2, 3 and 4, and on up to 19 and 20. Put the short leg in the top hole, and the long leg in the bottom hole. Look closely—the side with the short leg is flat around the base. It's important to install these correctly—they won't work if you put them in backward.

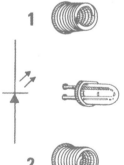

After you have stuck the legs of an LED through, flip the project board over and carefully bend the legs over toward the springs on either side. Then push the spring sideways to make an opening, stick the leg of the LED inside, and let go.

Got them all in? Good job. Double-check to make sure none of the LED wires are touching each other, or they won't work!

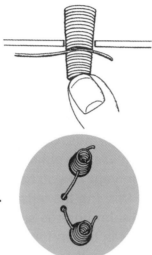

Part Two

The Resistors

Slow the Flow

Next, get out the resistors. They look like this:

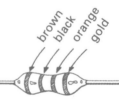

brown black orange gold

Resistors actually resist the flow of electrons. They are used to control how much electricity is traveling in a circuit, which is often very important. Their secret is the carbon inside of them. Carbon is a bad conductor, and only allows a small amount of electricity to flow through it. Resistors with different amounts of carbon inside can be used to allow different amounts of electricity to flow in a circuit.

Many of the components on your digital workbench need only a little bit of electricity to work. The battery produces more electricity than they need, and without resistors these parts would overheat and be ruined. You'd have fried chips!

Electricity straight from the battery would also make some circuits run too fast, but with a resistor, they slow down to a useful speed.

The goofy striped outfits on resistors are their code system. At first glance they all look alike, but the stripe combinations tell you just how much resistance each is willing (or able) to give. This resistance is measured in a unit called "ohms," named after a scientist named Georg Simon Ohm.

Time for a little resistance! There are two resistors with stripes that are brown, black, orange, and gold. These go into the places marked 10K on the project board (springs 55 and 56, plus 57 and 58). Press the legs through and bend them into the springs. It doesn't matter which way the legs are facing.

The resistor with the brown, black, yellow, and gold stripes goes in the spot marked 100K (springs 59 and 60). The last resistor, the one that is brown, black, green, and gold, goes in the slot marked 1 MEG (springs 61 and 62). Remember, with resistors, it doesn't matter which way you put them in.

Part Three

Capacitors

The Storage Tanks

Capacitors look like tiny soda cans with legs sticking out of the bottom. In a circuit, capacitors act like an electricity storage tank. Capacitors provide a place where electricity can be stored for a short time. The amount of electricity they can store is measured in units called "farads," which are named after a scientist by the name of Michael Faraday. Bigger capacitors can hold more charge and can let it out over a longer period of time than the little ones.

Sometimes electricity comes in pulses, and capacitors act like a shock absorber to smooth out variations in the electricity. They work together with a resistor to let out just the right amount of electricity.

There are two capacitors in your kit. Well, don't just read about them—go get them out of the box! If you look really closely, you can see there are numbers on the side. Find the one that says 1.0uF on it (that means 1 microfarad). Look for the minus sign on the side. Put the capacitor into the two small holes between springs 63 and 64, with the minus sign toward spring 64. Don't put it in backward, or it won't work!

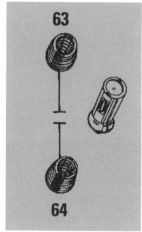

Next, take the other capacitor, which should say 10uF on it, and insert it into the small holes between springs 65 and 66, with the minus sign toward spring 66. Don't put it in backward, or it won't work! Nag, nag, nag . . . .

Part Four
Piezo Transducer

Make Some Noise

The piezo transducer is the flat, circular component about the size of a quarter. It's the noise maker in the crowd. "Piezo" is Greek for "pressure." Oh yeah, that's pronounced *pee-AY-zoh*. A transducer is something that can change one kind of energy into another.

The metal disk inside expands and contracts as pressure is put on it by electricity passing through it. So a piezo transducer changes electricity into sound waves—kind of like a speaker, only simpler.

Let's take a closer look. The piezo-electric disk expands when electricity flows through it, and contracts when the electricity stops. When the electricity oscillates—turns on and off and on and

off repeatedly—the disk bends out and in and out and in, which creates sound waves.

To install the piezo transducer insert the wires from the bottom of the disk through the holes next to springs 37 and 38. It doesn't matter which spring the wires connect to, just make sure the wires don't touch each other.

37

38

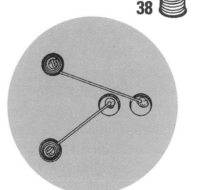

Part Five
The Push Button

Well, Push My Buttons!

When you press on the push button, you are connecting two springs together so that electricity can flow from one spring to the other. On your workbench, the push button is a simple piece of metal that is always connected to one spring, and when you push on the metal, it touches another spring. This makes a bridge to let the electricity go through. Release it and everything stops. No flow, no go.

Here's how to connect the push button: Find the small bent piece of metal, and, as shown, push it into spring 68, about halfway up the spring. The other end of the piece of metal should be over spring 67 but not touching it. When you push down on the piece of metal, you make a metal connection between springs 67 and 68.

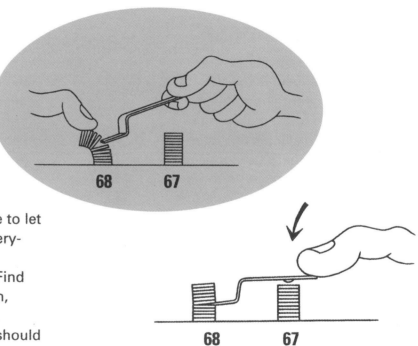

Part Six

Chips Ahoy!

Now It's Time to Install the Chips!

The NAND gate goes first. That's the one that makes all the decisions. It's the brains of the system. In fact, an entire computer could be built of just NAND gates. This one in your kit is called a quad NAND because it has four tiny little NAND gate circuits inside. These four gates make quite a hot team. It can make four on or off decisions at the same time—and it keeps on making them as fast as it gets an input. Each of the four NAND gates has two inputs and an output. In diagrams it looks like this:

Four gates times three legs accounts for 12 of the 14 legs you see. The other two connect the battery to the chip so electricity can get through the chip to make its decisions. For example, the legs that connect to springs 50 and 52 are the inputs to one of the gates. That's where the signal comes in. The leg that attaches to spring 48 is where the gate sends its answer, or "output." These messages control the other parts of the circuit board. Without the NAND gates, nothing would happen.

Most of what you see is just the package to hold a tiny piece of silicon with transistors in it. It's about 1/8 inch square. Each gate is made of 4 transistors for a total of 16 transistors. A home computer can have millions of transistors compactly nestled in silicon chips.

The NAND chip goes into the space on the bottom of the board. It's got 14 legs and the number  4011 printed on the front of the chip. On the back side of the front of the workbench (the side where you stuck lead wires into the springs) you'll see a NAND GATE above the rectangular hole. Place the circuit board in the hole so that the NAND gate chip fits in the hole. MAKE SURE THE TINY "UP" PRINTED IN THE CORNER OF THE CIRCUIT BOARD POINTS UP!

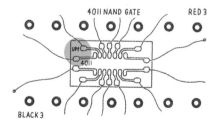

Find the two lead wires attached to the circuit board that have metal blobs on each end. The lead wire on the left attaches to the spring labeled

BLACK 3. To insert the metal blob into the spring, bend the spring over so there's enough room to get the metal blob in the spring, and then let go of the spring. The lead wire with metal blob on the right goes to the spring labeled RED 3. Now attach all the other lead wires to their corresponding springs (they're arranged in order). MAKE SURE NONE OF THE LEAD WIRES TOUCH!

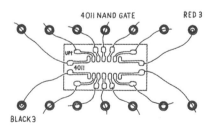

The Counter Chip

Next comes the Decade Counter Chip, or just "Counter Chip" for short. This is a chip you can count on. Actually that's all it does, is count. The thing that it counts, of course, is electrical signals. Each time the clock input leg—that's the one connected to spring 25—receives an ON signal the counter chip adds one to its total.

The clock signal sets the beat of the computer. It can tick millions of times per second. The counter in your electronic workbench will use a beat of 1 to 1,000 times per second, depending on the project.

So what about all those other legs?

Well, the input leg connected to spring 27 is called "STOP." It tells the chip to start or to stop counting. And the input leg connected to spring 23 resets the total to zero. The other 10 legs are the output legs, which output the 10 digits from 0 to 9. This is how it counts in binary. A counter chip is built up of a collection of logic gates like

your NAND gate, only it's got lots more gates (about 60) all laid out on a larger piece of silicon.

Now do the same installation for the counter chip as you did for the NAND gate chip. Place the circuit board in the hole labeled COUNTER. Again there are two lead wires with metal blobs, and these go into the springs labeled BLACK 2 and RED 2. As before, be certain no lead wires are touching each other!

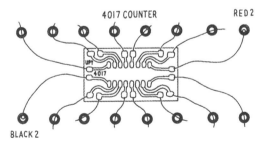

Part Seven
Power Up!

Now you need to attach some wires to the bottom of the project board. Get out the three red wires and three black wires (these wires have metal blobs at the ends).

Connect the long black wire from BLACK 1 to BLACK 2.

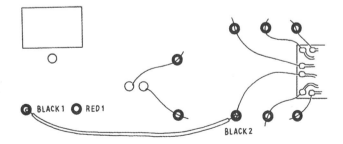

Make sure the metal blob is all the way in the spring. Now connect the short black wire from BLACK 2 to BLACK 3. Then connect the long red wire from RED 1 to RED 2, and the short red wire from RED 2 to RED 3.

Notice that these wires connect the battery and the chips. Remember from the "What Is Electricity?" section that there has to be a complete circuit to make electricity flow. Most projects will start and end at the battery terminals on top of the project board. There are a few projects where both battery terminals don't get connected from the top. But have no fear—the battery and chips will always be connected from underneath.

Part Eight
Battery's Up!

The battery connector looks like this:

Starting from the front side, run the wires into the hole next to springs 39 and 40. The red wire connects to spring 39, and the black wire connects to spring 40. MAKE SURE YOU GET THE WIRES CON-NECTED TO THE RIGHT SPRINGS! Underneath, next to the springs, you will see RED and BLACK for the correct springs to attach the wires.

That's it—you're done!
Carefully fold the cardboard together, and your workbench is complete. Congratulations! Don't break your arm patting yourself on the back—you haven't made the projects yet.

Now let's have some real fun as you become a Digital Wizard!

Testing Your Electronic Workbench

Yeah! Your workbench is complete. But does it work? To be on the safe side, assemble a simple circuit that will prove once and for all—beyond a shadow of a doubt—that your workbench is in premier working order. In addition, if you follow these basic rules of wiring, you're less likely to have problems with your circuits.

Basic Rules of Wiring

1. Connect metal to metal. Make sure the wire (not the plastic) is hooked into the spring.
2. Never connect both ends of an LED directly to the battery or the LED will burn out.
3. Try not to bend the wires more than you have to. Eventually they will break.
4. Use the shortest wire possible. You may need a longer one somewhere else, and besides, it looks tidier.
5. Last, but certainly not least, never hook up the battery until you have the whole circuit completed. You could fry your components!

Warning!
Do not use any other source of electricity with your projects. The current from wall sockets or appliances is very, very—I repeat VERY!—strong and can cause you great injury!

Warning!
Do not just connect the two terminals of the battery directly together with a piece of wire or other metal. The battery and wire could heat up enough to burn you!

Test Circuit #1: The LEDs

This test circuit will determine if you hooked up everything right. You didn't put the LEDs in backward? Did you?

Here's how to build your test circuit: Connect the bare wire to springs 1, 3, 5, 7, 9, 11, 13, 15, 17, and 19. This bare wire stays in place for most of the projects. Then hook up a yellow wire to spring #46 (just let it hang out for now). Hook up the following pairs of springs: 42 to 44, ~~44~~ to 40, and 40 to 19. Hook up the battery. 54   and 41 to 39

Remember! The battery gets connected *after* you have made all the hookups.

Once you're connected, take the loose end of the hanging yellow wire (it's hooked up to spring 46, remember?) and touch it to each lower LED spring (2, 4, 6, 8, 10, 12, 14, 16, 18, and 20) to test your workbench. Conveniently, this will also show whether you put any LEDs in backward.

Test Circuit #2: The Resistor

Let's try another one.

Clear your workbench. You might as well leave that bare wire in springs 1, 3, 5, 7, 9, 11, 13, 15, 17, and 19. You're gonna need it for this one, too. Now connect 19 to 40, 39 to 57, and 58 to a yellow wire. Connect the battery. Touch the yellow wire from 58 to each lower LED spring (2, 4, 6, 8, 10, 12, 14, 16, 18, and 20). If your resistors are wired correctly, each LED will give off a faint light as its spring is touched.

Troubleshooting

OK, so you've run across a circuit that just isn't cooperating. There's no doubt you've done everything right and you've double-checked all the connections. Sometimes when circuits are cranky, the best thing to do is to pull all the wires and start over. Believe me, it's much easier than trying to trace a miswired wire.

So you've rewired it, and still nothing's happening. It could be the battery. Do Test Circuit #1 (page 27). If none of the LEDs light, try a new nine-volt battery. If some of them light, replace the LEDs that don't.

Test the resistors. Do Test Circuit #2 (page 27). If each LED doesn't give off a faint light when its spring is touched, it could be a resistor. Try a different resistor by removing the wires from 57 and 58 and putting them into 55 and 56.

Check all the connections. Make sure the wires are securely pinched by the springs.

If things still aren't working, there's one more place to look. Check underneath the electronic workbench. Make sure no bare wires are crossing or touching each other. Look very closely at the wires coming from the computer chips. They've been voted most likely to be touching each other. The wires from the piezo transducer could easily be touching each other, too. If wires are touching and you just can't seem to separate them, wrap a little piece of tape around one of the wires. This will act as an insulator for that wire.

What's a Schematic?

What's that picture in the corner? Good question. Take a look at the projects starting on page 32. Most of them have a picture in the corner showing a diagram for that circuit.

There is a connection diagram that goes along with each project. (That's the picture in the corner that looks like a map.) Each of the symbols is like the symbols on your workbench. They are all connected to show which way the electricity flows making that circuit work. In the diagram (just like on your workbench), the components are shown with these symbols:

Piezo, resistor, capacitor, pushbutton, counter chip, NAND gate, LED, and the battery. Look for these symbols on your workbench.

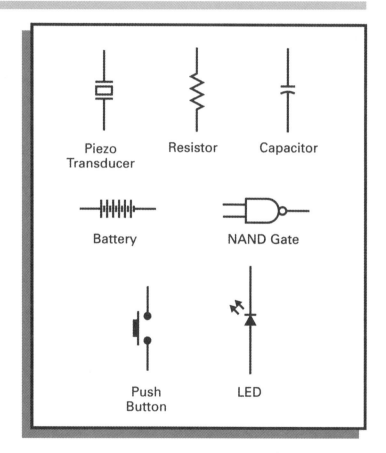

Piezo Transducer   Resistor   Capacitor

Battery   NAND Gate

Push Button   LED

Note to Parents

Good job of not assembling the Electronic Workbench for your child. As torturous as it is to watch, you both learn more if your kid does the work. (Besides, you could do the projects after your child has gone to bed.)

LEDs, capacitors, and most of the components in this workbench are available at your local Radio Shack or other electronic parts store. Individually, the components are inexpensive, so if one breaks, don't fret.

Your main job is to be moral support. Practice these phrases: "Good job" and "Maybe you could try this . . ."

If a project absolutely will not cooperate, skip it. Have your child do a different one. Even though they're nonhuman, computer components can be just as temperamental as any human. Don't let these get the best of you or your kid. Remember, you can always disconnect the battery and walk away! Have Fun!

EXPERIMENT 1

AND Gate

This circuit will light up the number "1" LED.

After you make all the connections, take each of the two wires and touch them both to spring 41. When you touch one loose wire AND the other loose wire to spring 41, the LED will light up.

Here's how to build an AND GATE: Connect the bare wire to springs 1, 3, 5, 7, 9, 11, 13, 15, 17, and 19. Then hook up 43-55, 45-57, 56-58, 54-56, 47-51, 51-53, 49-2, 19-40, a long yellow wire to 43, and a long yellow wire to 45.

Remember! The battery gets connected *after* you have made all the hookups.

What's Going On?

You've just constructed the AND gate. Congratulations! Now what's an "AND gate"? Remember in the introduction (you did read the introduction, didn't you?) we said that gates are the decision makers in a computer. They take in information as either "yes" or "no" and give out, or "output" (in computer lingo), information as "yes" or "no."

The output on this gate is the "1" LED. The two loose wires from 43 AND 45 are the inputs in your AND gate. When they aren't touching

anything, both inputs are zero, or "no," and the
output of the AND gate is zero and the LED is off.
When they both touch spring 41 they pick up electrical current and the input is one, or "yes" and the
AND gate is one and the LED lights. What happens
when only one of the wires touches 41? Try it.
Right! It doesn't light the LED.

Let's check out an example of an AND gate. Sue
and Kevin are each an input to the gate. Their mom
wants them to go play catch. Both Sue AND Kevin
have to play catch before the game can happen.
Let's chart all the possibilities of ways this could go.
Sue says no and Kevin says no, so they don't play.
(But at least they're happy about it!) The next line
down shows that Sue doesn't want to play, but
Kevin does—they don't play and Kevin's bummed.
Look at the Truth Table to see other possibilities.

I'll bet you have an AND gate in your kitchen.
Think of a small appliance that has to have both the
door shut AND the "start" button pushed in order
for it to work. No, not the automatic potato peeler.
It's the microwave! A microwave oven is like an

AND gate; it needs both the door closed AND the
"start" button pressed for the oven to go on.

OR Gate

This circuit turns on the "1" LED.

Make sure the workbench is cleared off and the battery is disconnected.

Here are the connections for your OR gate: Connect the bare wire to springs 1, 3, 5, 7, 9, 11, 13, 15, 17, and 19. Then hook up 43-45, 45-55, 47-52, 51-53, 49-50, 53-57, 56-58, 54-56, 48-2, 19-40, a long yellow wire to 43, and a long yellow wire to 51.

Since this is an OR gate, input from one wire OR the other one will complete the circuit. Give it a try. After hooking up the battery, touch one of the hanging yellow wires to 41 and see what happens. Does the LED light? Now touch the other wire to 41 without the first one getting in the way. If it lights, you're there!

What's Going On?

This gate is the least picky of all the gates. The OR gate will have a "yes" output if one input OR the other is "yes." Let's check out Catlin and Alec. They've both been asked to take out the trash. A "yes" input from either of them would get the trash out. On the chart it looks like this.

How many combinations would get the garbage emptied? According to the chart there are three different ways to get that trash emptied. That's enough to make any parent happy.

The output on this gate is the LED. When it's off, the output is "no." When it's on, the output is "yes." The two loose wires are the inputs in your OR gate. When they aren't touching anything, the input is zero, or "no." When you touch either of them to spring 41, they pick up electrical current, and the input is one, or "yes."

Another example of an OR gate can be found simply by opening the door in a car. Let's say that the output happens when the interior light goes on. You'll notice that the light goes on when one door OR the other is open. It also goes on when both doors are open.

NAND Gate

NO+NO=YES
NO+YES=YES
YES+NO=YES
YES+YES=NO

The output on this circuit is the number "1" LED. When it is off, the output is "no." When it is on, the output is "yes."

Make sure the workbench is cleared off and the battery is disconnected.

Here are the connections for your NAND gate: Connect the bare wire to springs 1, 3, 5, 7, 9, 11, 13, 15, 17, and 19. Hook up 43-55, 45-57, 56-58, 54-56, 47-2, 19-40, a long yellow wire to 43, and a long yellow wire to 45.

Touch the two loose wires to spring 41. When both inputs are on, the output is off. Touch no wires to spring 41, and the LED is lit, making the output of the gate "yes." Touch only one of the wires, and the lights remain lit. Touch both wires, and the LED turns off, making the output of the gate "no." The only way to make this gate output "no" is to have both inputs "yes" at the same time.

What's Going On?

This circuit is the exact opposite of the AND gate—it's the Not AND gate, or NAND gate for short. If both inputs are "yes," then the output is "no." If one or both inputs are "no," then the output is "yes." (Stubborn things!)

The NAND gate is the basic logic gate used in computers. Look at the NAND gates on your workbench. You'll be using them a lot.

An example of two things happening in order to stop an output is when you buckle up for safety in your car. You know that loud obnoxious noise that buzzes unmercifully until you buckle your seat belt? To shut off that noise, both people in the front seat have to have seat belts on. If only one or the other buckles up, the noise stays on. Unless, of course, you wait 30 seconds or so and the buzzer gives up on you and goes off.

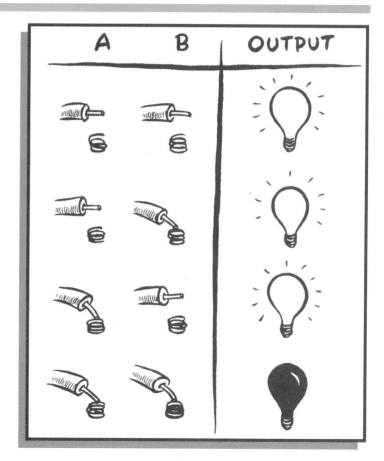

XOR Gate

The Exclusive OR gate, or the XOR gate, only has a "yes" output if one OR the other inputs is "yes." If they're both "no" or both "yes," then the output is "no." It's a little pickier than a plain OR gate.

Here are the connections: Connect the bare wire to springs 1, 3, 5, 7, 9, 11, 13, 15, 17, and 19. Then hook up 55-53, 51-52-57, 54-56, 56-58, 53-43, 49-45-50, 42-47, 48-44, 46-2, 19-40, a long yellow wire to 55, and a long yellow wire to 57.

O.K., I DECIDE WHO GETS IN AND WHO DOESN'T

What's Going On?

Check out the Truth Table of an Exclusive OR gate. You or your brother were both invited to go to the movies. There's just one problem—your mom has only one extra ticket. And because she doesn't want to hurt anybody's feelings, you can go if your brother doesn't want to, or your brother can go if you don't want to, but if you and your brother both want to go, then she won't take either one of you.

The output on the gate you've constructed is the number 1 LED. When it is off, the output is "no." When it is on, the output is "yes."

The two loose wires are the inputs in your XOR gate. When they aren't touching anything, the input is zero, or "no." When you touch them to spring 41, they pick up some electrical current, and then the input is one, or "yes."

If you don't touch any wires to spring 41, the LED is off. The  output of the gate is "no." Touch one wire or the other, and the light is lit. The output of the gate is "yes."

If you touch both wires, the LED turns off. The output of the gate is again "no." The only way to make this gate output "yes" is to have one or the other of the inputs "yes," but not both at the same time.

There you have it—the four gates you've just constructed make up most of the simple yes-or-no decisions that happen millions of times a second to make computers do really cool things.

Vote Counter

This circuit has three wires that just hang out waiting to cast their vote. When the circuit is complete, you will touch the three yellow wires to the battery to light the LED.

Make sure the workbench is cleared off and the battery is disconnected.

Here are the connections to make your Vote Counter: Connect the bare wire to springs 1, 3 ,5, 7 ,9 ,11, 13, 15, 17, and 19. Then hook up 42-56-yellow wire, 46-50-52, 44-58-yellow wire, 48-53, 43-45, 45-49, 47-2, 51-60-yellow wire, 55-57-59, 59-40, 19-40.

What's Going On?

Once the battery is hooked up and all the wires are in place, touch a yellow wire to spring number 39 to vote yes. Remember that each wire has to touch the spring to cast a vote.

All in favor say "Aye!" (That's pronounced "I" for you phonetic spellers out there.)

You've just made yourself a vote counter. However, the catch is that the vote has to be unanimous—which means everyone has to agree or the vote doesn't count. In computer terms this is called a 3-input AND gate. All three inputs have to be "yes" to complete the circuit.

Get two other friends together, each holding a probe. If there are just two of you, take the extra wire and attach it to spring 39—that will make it appear to the circuit that the third person is always voting "yes!" Pose the question: Is pizza your favorite food? Each answer the question with a Yes vote by touching the yellow wire to spring 39. If the answer is No, just sit there and don't touch the spring. See how many of the following questions you and your friends answer unanimously. (No cheating!)

Do you like staying up late at night?
Do you really like school?
Do you have enough clothes?
Should there be more Saturdays in a week?

Get the hang of the game? Now you and your friends can make up more questions and test yourselves.

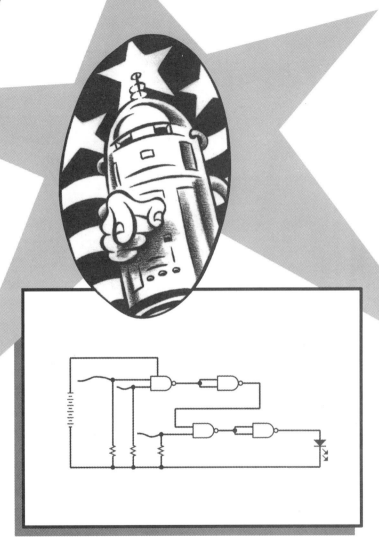

Flip-Flop

This circuit will make four LEDs go on when you press the push button. They'll go off when you push it again.

Clear off ALL wires from your workbench and make sure the battery is disconnected.

Remove the bare wire from 1, 3 , 5, 7, 9, 11, 13, 15, 17, 19. You don't need it for this one. Then connect 42-47, 44-48, 2-46-50, 43-45-24, 52-49, 51-53-26, 39-67, 27-36, 23-28, 25-59-63-68, 60-64-40-7, 1-4, 3-6, 5-8.

What's Going On?

In this circuit, one signal turns the LEDs on. They will remember to stay on until you push the button and turn the LEDs off. (Just don't wait so long that the battery drains—then they'll go off permanently!)

Big deal, four LEDs go on. Yeah, it is a BIG deal! The flip-flop is the short-term memory of the computer—which is of primo importance to a computer. It's the biggest deal there is to a computer.

Everything you type into the computer is in flip-flops and will stay there until you close that document. Once it's closed, you've turned off those flip-flops, erasing everything you've done.

THE FLIP-FLOP CIRCUIT IN ACTION

Now, how do we turn it on?

The flip-flop is like the Power button on your TV (or remote as the case may be). Push it once and it turns the TV ON. Wait until *Star Trek* is over, push it again and the TV goes off. The flip-flop remembers that you turned on the TV, and now must turn it off.

Save Your Work!

Did you turn off the computer before saving that 10-page book report? OOPS! You've flipped off your flip-flops. Sorry, your work's gone, never to be retrieved again. The "Save" command takes your work from the flip-flops and puts it on the hard drive. This important act commits your stuff to the computer's permanent memory until you change it, add to it, or delete it.

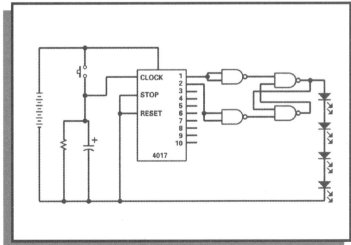

Push Button Counter

To make the counter go up by one, press the push button. The next LED lights up! Each time you press the button, the next LED will light up.

Clear off the wires from your workbench and make sure the battery is disconnected.

Here are the connections: Connect the bare wire to springs 1, 3, 5, 7, 9, 11, 13, 15, 17, and 19. Then hook up 19-40, 52-50-43-49, 25-48, 51-55-39, 53-57-66, 56-67-63-45, 58-68-64-40, 65-47, 22-12, 24-4, 26-2, 28-6, 32-16, 34-8, 35-18, 33-10, 31-20, 30-14, 36-27-23.

What's Going On?

The counter goes up by one when you press the push button. The first LED should light up! Each time you press the button, the next LED will light up. If you get a nice steady rhythm going, your button-pushing acts as a "clock" for the circuit. This is how clocks that are built into computers work, except for the little fact that the computer clocks click away at about 40 or 50 million times a second.

In many digital devices, a vibrating crystal does the clicking to keep track of the time.

Alright, let's go, your time's up!

Now Try This

Rewire your circuit to count to the first six lights and then start all over. Here's what you do. Disconnect the battery and then remove the wire from 30 to 14. Also remove the wire from 23 to 27. Connect a wire from 23 to 30 and reconnect the battery. Now press the push button and see what happens after the sixth LED lights up. Yeah, it goes back to "1" and starts over.

Now you have the circuits to make a digital clock. Go look at the minutes on a digital clock. One column counts to 10 and one column only counts to 6. How come? The column on the right goes from 0 to 9. That's 10 digits. The column on the left goes from 0 to 5. That's 6 digits! Once the clock reads 59 minutes, it goes back to "00."

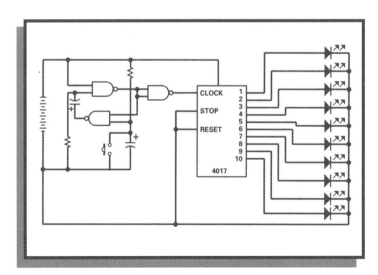

Flashing Lights

This flashy circuit will get the LEDs flashing one right after the other.

Clear off the wires from your workbench and make sure the battery is disconnected.

Connect the bare wire to springs 1, 3, 5, 7, 9, 11, 13, 15, 17, and 19. Then hook up 26-2, 24-4, 28-6, 34-8, 33-10, 22-12, 30-14, 32-16, 35-18, 31-53, 53-51, 49-45-43, 47-20, 31-37, 38-40-19, 42-44-63-55, 52-50-46-56, 23-27-36, 25-48-64.

What's Going On?

Well, this circuit is a real flasher! Once it's hooked up, it goes through the whole series of LEDs one at a time.

That's the piezo transducer keeping that nice rhythmic pace that you hear each time the last LED lights.

The NAND gate creates an oscillator which flip-flops back and forth to create a pulse of electricity. Every time the NAND gate flips from off to on, the counter counts up one, and the next LED lights up.

So where would you find all this flashiness? You probably see it so much that you don't even notice. You know that last

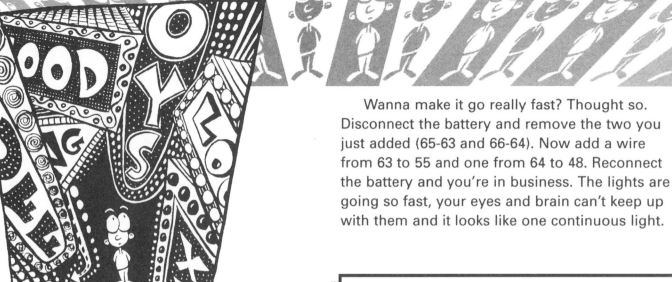

Wanna make it go really fast? Thought so. Disconnect the battery and remove the two you just added (65-63 and 66-64). Now add a wire from 63 to 55 and one from 64 to 48. Reconnect the battery and you're in business. The lights are going so fast, your eyes and brain can't keep up with them and it looks like one continuous light.

billboard you passed, or that sign in the toy store window? Flashing lights around your favorite pizza sign put that pizza in your face.

Now Try This

Let's slow this circuit down a little. Disconnect the battery and add a wire connecting 65 to 63, and one from 66 to 64. Now reconnect the battery. You just slowed down your circuit by adding another capacitor. (Remember, that's the electrical storage bucket.)

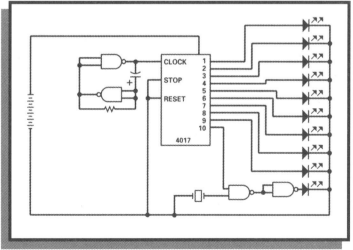

EEEENY, MEENY, MINEY, MOE...

Random Number Generator

In this circuit you will press the push button to make an LED light up. But the LEDs will light up randomly, so you won't know which LED will stay lit until you press the button.

Clear off the wires from your workbench and make sure the battery is disconnected.

Here are the connections: Connect the bare wire to springs 1, 3, 5, 7, 9, 11, 13, 15, 17, and 19. Then hook up 42-44-56-63, 46-55-50-52, 64-48-25, 2-26, 18-24, 8-28, 12-34, 20-33, 4-22, 16-30, 10-32, 6-35, 14-31, 23-36, 19-40-57, 27-67-58, 39-68.

Remember to connect the battery.

What's Going On?

Are the lights blinking uncontrollably? Good. That's just what they're supposed to do. Now when you press the push button the lights stop blinking and one will remain on—that's your random number. Release the push button and the blinking starts all over again.

Ever play computer games where you never know what's going to pop up where? Just like your video games, your circuit is running through a list of numbers with no regular order.

What's happening is the counter is sending signals to the LEDs in a normal sequence, but the wires connecting the counter to the LEDs are all mixed up. That makes the lights flash in what seems to be a random pattern. When you press the push button, the flashing stops with one light left on.

Now Try This

Use your random numbers to play "Freeze It!"

The object of the game is to freeze the LED (press the push button) only on even numbers. You get seven tries. The one who gets the most even numbers in seven freezes is the winner. Sharpen your button-pushing finger and GO!

Another rule you can use to play Freeze It is to see if you can add up to exactly 20 with your freezes. For example, freezing it on 4, 7, and 9 makes you a winner. Six, eight, and nine equal twenty-three—that's too high. You lose! Make up new rules—just make sure you and your friends are playing with the same rules at the same time.

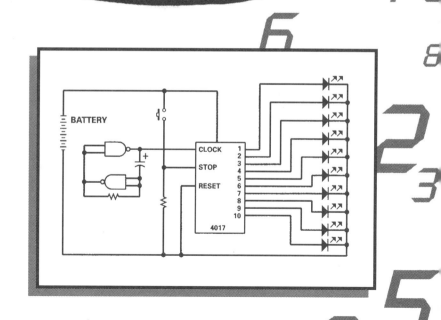

Light Trap!

When you hook up this circuit the LEDs will flash in a row. It will look like they're zooming by, but this string of lights has a catch. It has been designed to have the lights go out when you press the button exactly when the number 5 LED is lit. Hitting any other number just causes that particular number to light up.

Here are the connections for your Light Trap game: Connect the bare wire to springs 1, 3, 5 ,7, 9, 11, 13, 15, 17, and 19. Then hook up 42-44-56, 46-55-50-52, 25-48-64, 2-26, 4-24, 6-28, 8-34, 53-10-33, 12-22, 14-30, 16-32, 18-35, 20-31, 23-36, 47-19, 43-45-49, 27-51-59-68, 60-40, 67-39, 44-63, 60-66, 65-68.

If it's going too fast, you may want to practice at a slower pace. To do that, take the wire out of #56 and put it into #58. Add a separate small wire connecting 56 to 57. Now you can play Light Trap at a more reasonable speed.

What's Going On?

This circuit is working to measure how good your timing is. Just like when you play a video game you often have to push the button at just the right time. In one of those games it might be when to jump from an airplane to stomp on a bug. With this project the idea is to watch those blinking little lights and try to catch the exact time the #5 LED lights up. Your goal is to push the push button at that exact moment! When you get it, the flashing stops.

Here's how to play Light Trap. After you hook up all the wires and the battery, the lights will be flashing. Watch the pace closely for a few rounds and get ready to strike. Can you see individual lights light up, or does it look like one big blur? If you push the button just as the #5 LED lights up, the row of lights goes off and you win! Challenge your friends to see who can turn lights off the most times in one minute.

This is good practice for your hand-eye coordination (or uncoordination, as the case may be).

Timing has to be just right with your trigger finger to get the whole row to black out.

Would this be a good example of an OR gate or an AND gate? If you said AND gate, you're a champ. To get the desired output (lights out), the #5 has to be lit AND you have to push the button.

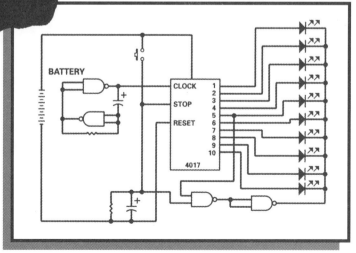

51

Light Chaser

In this circuit every third LED will light. It will cycle through all the LEDs and it will buzz at the first one.

To make your Light Chaser circuit, connect the bare wire to springs 1, 3 ,5, 7, 9, 11, 13, 15, 17, and 19. Then hook up 42-44-57-65, 58-46-50-52-51-53, 66-48-25, 49-37, 38-40-19, 26-2-8-14, 24-4-10-16, 28-6-12-18, 34-23, 36-27.

What's Going On?

This circuit looks as if the lights are chasing each other. Well, in a way they are. They're arranged to flash in a sequence. Every third LED lights. Then the second third, then the third third. Look at it to see what I mean. Marquees at movie theaters flash in a patterned sequence such as surrounding the name of the current box office hit.

The secret here is that the outputs of the counter are hooked up to three LEDs at the same time. So you get more than you bargained for. The counter is hooked up to LEDs 1, 4, and 7. Then in the next pulse it is hooked up to 2, 5, and 8. The third then is, yeah, you got it, 3, 6, and 9. So the output from the counter shows that the first set goes on and off, then the second set goes on and off, followed by the third set.

Look closely at your circuit. Can you see this pattern of lights move?

The impression that the lights are moving is called "persistence of vision." The lights flash on and off so fast that your brain can't get rid of the first set before the second lights come into view. This is how cartoons, TV, and computer animation work. The pictures change so fast that they create the illusion of continuous movement and you see Mickey or *Toy Story*.

Now Try This

You can do your own persistence-of-vision effect. Wiggle your index finger back and forth in front of you very quickly. It looks like you have lots of fingers.

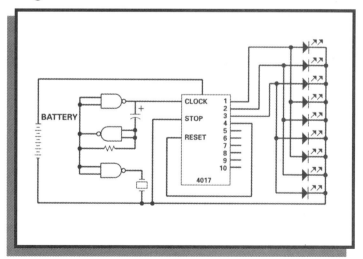

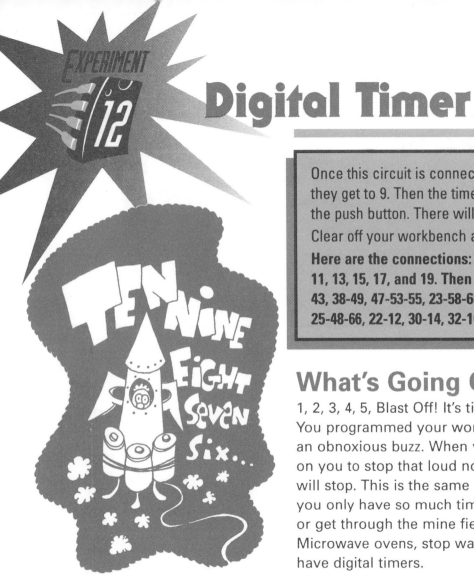

Digital Timer

Once this circuit is connected, the LEDs will light up one at a time until they get to 9. Then the timer will buzz and keep buzzing until you press the push button. There will be a few seconds between each light.

Clear off your workbench and make sure the battery is disconnected.

Here are the connections: Connect the bare wire to springs 1, 3, 5, 7, 9, 11, 13, 15, 17, and 19. Then hook up 42-44-60-65, 46-50-52-59, 37-56-45-43, 38-49, 47-53-55, 23-58-68, 39-67, 57-40-19, 2-26, 4-24, 6-28, 8-34, 10-33, 25-48-66, 22-12, 30-14, 32-16, 35-18, 31-27-51.

What's Going On?

1, 2, 3, 4, 5, Blast Off! It's timer time! You've just made a digital timer. You programmed your workbench to count up to 9 and then to make an obnoxious buzz. When you have enough people ready to pounce on you to stop that loud noise, press the push button and the noise will stop. This is the same kind of timer used in video games where you only have so much time to grab the treasure, stomp the monster, or get through the mine field before you're eaten by a baboon. Microwave ovens, stop watches at basketball games—lots of things have digital timers.

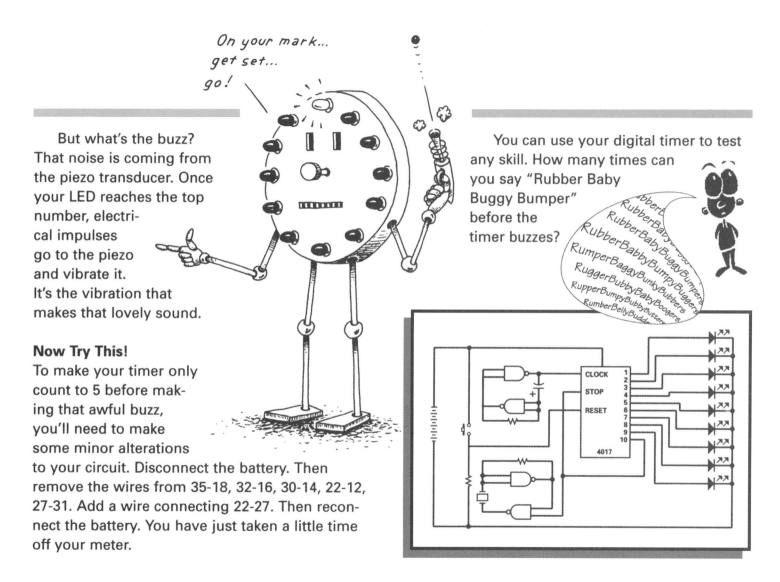

But what's the buzz? That noise is coming from the piezo transducer. Once your LED reaches the top number, electrical impulses go to the piezo and vibrate it. It's the vibration that makes that lovely sound.

Now Try This!

To make your timer only count to 5 before making that awful buzz, you'll need to make some minor alterations to your circuit. Disconnect the battery. Then remove the wires from 35-18, 32-16, 30-14, 22-12, 27-31. Add a wire connecting 22-27. Then reconnect the battery. You have just taken a little time off your meter.

On your mark... get set... go!

You can use your digital timer to test any skill. How many times can you say "Rubber Baby Buggy Bumper" before the timer buzzes?

Reaction Timer

This circuit tests how quickly you react to a series of LEDs blinking really fast. To build it, clear off the wires from the workbench and make sure the battery is disconnected.

This is how the wires get connected: Connect the bare wire to springs 1, 3, 5, 7, 9, 11, 13, 15, and 17, NOT 19. Be sure that you DON'T connect 19. Then hook up 42-44-58-63, 46-55-50-52, 56-57, 64-48-25, 2-26, 4-24, 6-28, 8-34, 10-33, 12-22, 14-30, 16-32, 18-35, 60-62-66-40-17, 23-20-59, 27-19-61-65-68, 67-39, 59-yellow wire.

To test your reaction time, take the end of the yellow wire attached to 59 and touch it to spring 39. This resets the circuit, and the lights will stop blinking. In about 4 seconds, they'll start again. Press the push button to make the lights stop and test how fast your reaction is. See if you can push it before the lights reach the end of the row!

What's Going On?

Reaction time! When would you need to test how fast you can react to something? Well, playing video games, of course! Using the ability of digital circuits to measure time very accurately, games track how

quickly you respond. They use your reaction time to decide if you win or lose. Good luck!

Reaction timers are also used to test your hand-eye coordination or to quickly your muscles can react.

You're at the starting line. BAM! Th off. You run like mad to the finish line. tion time gets you running as soon as you hear that noise—no sooner, no later. You're a winner!

Now Try This

If you want to speed up your reaction timer to test your now-sharpened skills, first disconnect the battery. Remove the wire connecting 56 to 57. Then take both wires from 58 and put them into 56. This removes a resistor from the circuit, allowing more electricity to get through. Hey! We already talked about resistors in the introduction, so this is a good time to show that they really do their job.

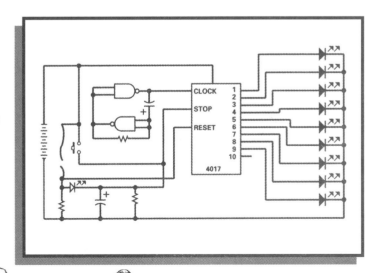

Sound-Activated Counter

After you hook up the circuit, give one hard clap over the piezo transducer. One LED will light. Each clap lights the next LED on your board.

Clear off the wires from your workbench and make sure the battery is disconnected.

Here are the connections for your sound-activated counter: Connect the bare wire to springs 1, 3, 5, 7, 9, 11, 13, 15, 17, and 19. Then hook up 42-47-59, 25-44-48, 46-65, 50-56-66, 52-41, 43-45-58-60, 37-55-40-19, 26-2, 24-4, 28-6, 34-8, 33-10, 22-12, 30-14, 32-16, 35-18, 31-20, 23-27-36, 57-38.

What's Going On?

Ever seen those TV ads for the sound-activated light switches? Or how about the key chain where you clap and it beeps? Those circuits work similarly to your circuit, but instead of just turning on and off, your clapping sound will run a counting circuit. Pretty cool, huh?

In this circuit, the signal to light the next light is coming from the piezo (pee-AY-zo) transducer, which is made up of a special crystalline material. When you clap over the piezo transducer, the sound waves push on the crystals. The stress in the crystals produces electricity. In Greek the word "piezo" means "pressure."

Where is that pressure coming from? The sound of your clapping makes sound waves, and the sound waves press against the surface of the piezo transducer. The electricity produced by the pressure sends a signal to the counter. Each clap sends a new signal. The counter receives the signal and lights the next LED.

How softly can you clap and still pick up the sound? What happens if you shout or talk into the piezo? Does your voice make enough vibration to send a signal to the counter? Does it work if you tap your finger on the piezo?

I heard that...

Now Try This!

To make the piezo more sensitive, disconnect the battery and let's change a few wires. Remove the wire from #59 and put it into #61. Also take the wire out of #60 and stick it into #62. Reconnect the battery and you're in business. Is the piezo sensitive enough to pick up a whisper or a light tap?

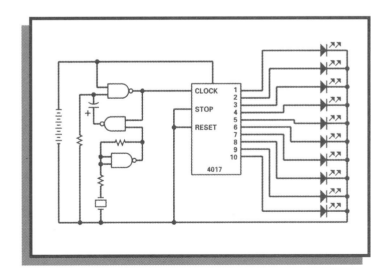

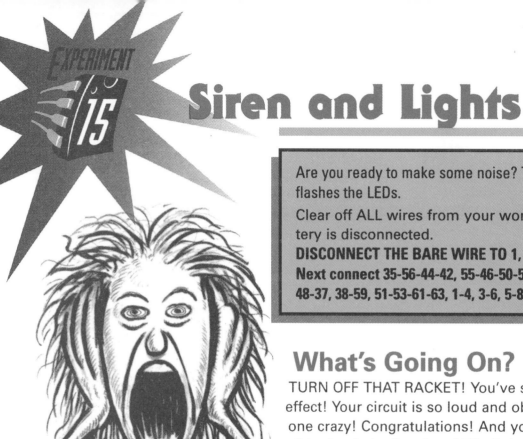

Siren and Lights

Are you ready to make some noise? This circuit makes noises and flashes the LEDs.

Clear off ALL wires from your workbench and make sure the battery is disconnected.

DISCONNECT THE BARE WIRE TO 1, 3 ,5, 7, 9, 11, 13, 15, 17 and 19. Next connect 35-56-44-42, 55-46-50-52, 2-25-43-45-49-62, 10-47-60-64, 48-37, 38-59, 51-53-61-63, 1-4, 3-6, 5-8, 7-15-40, 9-12, 11-14, 13-16.

What's Going On?

TURN OFF THAT RACKET! You've succeeded in getting the desired effect! Your circuit is so loud and obnoxious that you're driving someone crazy! Congratulations! And you have blinking LEDs to boot! In this circuit the first four LEDs light to one sound and the second four LEDs light to a different tone. It's loud enough to wake up the dead. Aren't you glad your alarm clock doesn't sound like this?

NOW HEAR THIS! EEEeeeeEEEEeeee!!!! Ambulances, police cars, even smoke alarms all use these loud tones to move in on the other noises that are filling your head! Usually this kind of siren-and-light combo is used in an emergency situation.

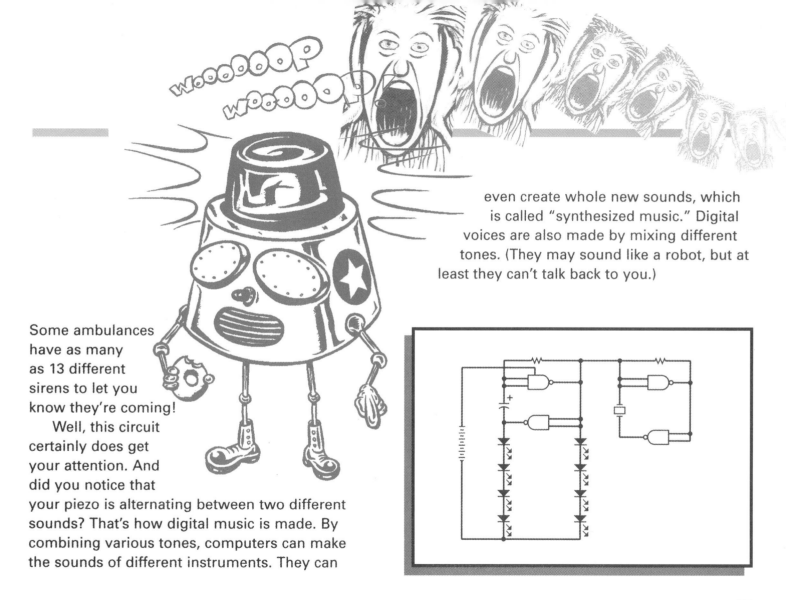

even create whole new sounds, which is called "synthesized music." Digital voices are also made by mixing different tones. (They may sound like a robot, but at least they can't talk back to you.)

Some ambulances have as many as 13 different sirens to let you know they're coming! Well, this circuit certainly does get your attention. And did you notice that your piezo is alternating between two different sounds? That's how digital music is made. By combining various tones, computers can make the sounds of different instruments. They can

Digital Resistance Checker

Clear off the wires from your workbench and make sure the battery is disconnected.

Here are the connections: Connect the bare wire to springs 1, 3, 5, 7, 9, 11, 13, 15, 17, and 19. Then hook up 42-44-56-63, 55-52-50-46, 25-48-64, yellow wire-51-53-62, 49-19, 31-57, yellow wire-65-58, 66-40, 39-61, 23-27-36, 26-2, 24-4, 28-6, 34-8, 33-10, 22-12, 30-14, 32-16, 35-18.

When you hook up the battery, the LEDs will light. Touch the two yellow wires together and the lights go out.

I'm CONDUCTING!

What's Going On?

So you think you're pretty hot stuff, huh? Well, this circuit proves that you are! You're actually conducting electricity. How electrifying! This digital circuit measures how well different materials conduct electricity. You included!

Squeeze the end of each of the yellow wires with your fingers. You should be able to squeeze hard enough to turn the LEDs off. If it doesn't work, lick your fingers before squeezing. (You won't get shocked—honest!!)

If there is a lot of resistance in the circuit, lots of the lights will stay on. The lower the resistance, the more lights will go off.

When you squeeze the wire, you lower the resistance in the circuit, and more lights go out. The electricity is going through your body. Yeah, your skin conducts electricity. (Ever gotten shocked after rubbing your feet on a carpet? Zap! Oh, I hate that.) The more you squeeze, the better connection you make between your skin and the wire. Water helps make an even better connection.

Now Try This

Take two wads of aluminum foil and stick one end of a yellow wire in each of the wads. Squeeze the foil. As you squeeze harder, more lights should go out. See if you can squeeze and release pres-

sure and get two lights to light, then five lights. Play with the resistance and watch the lights dance at your command.

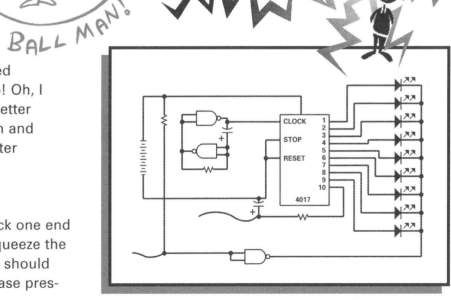

Digital Dice

Place the Digital Dice overlay over LEDs 1–6.
Connect the bare wire to springs 1, 3, 5, 7, 9, 11, 13, 15, 17, and 19. Then hook up 63-57-55-44-42, 58-56-52-50-46, 48-64-68, 60-40-19, 25-59-67, 2-26, 4-24, 6-28, 8-34, 10-33, 12-22, 23-30.
Press the push button to make dice 1-6 light randomly.

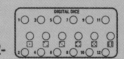

What's Going On?

Roll 'em! You've just made yourself a dice game. Way to go! When you hold down the push button, all six LEDs blink randomly until you take your finger off the button. When you press the button, it stops on any one of those six dice. And your number's up!

This is a similar circuit to the Random Number Generator. This one gives the last four LEDs a break.

Now Try This

Wanna play "Fifty"? It's an old dice game where doubles is the only thing that scores. You get doubles by, of course, lighting the

same die twice in a row. Here are the rules. The first player takes two presses. Lighting two ones, two twos, two fours, or two fives scores you five points. Two sixes earns you 25 points. However, when a player lights two threes, he or she loses all the points scored up to that point in the game. Yep, you start back at zero. For throwing anything other than a matching pair, there's no score and no penalty. The first player to score 50 points wins. Good luck!

Let's Play "Sevens"!

The object is to get as many sevens as possible in 10 turns. A turn is two presses. The first player takes a turn and adds up the total of the two dice. Seven is worth a point. Any other total isn't worth anything, but in either case your turn is up. The next player takes two presses and adds the total. The one who has the most sevens after 10 rounds is the winner.

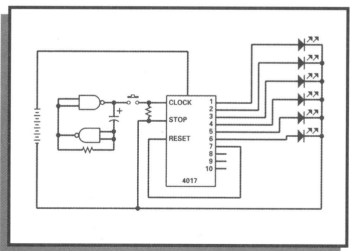

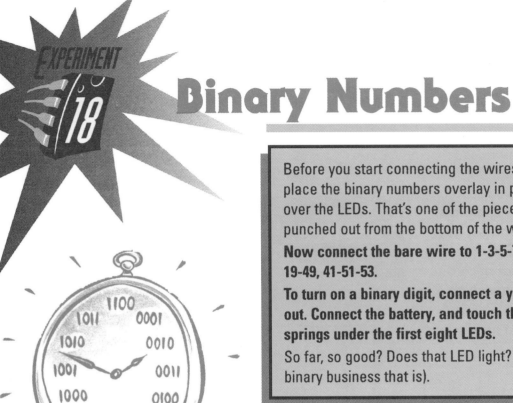

Binary Numbers

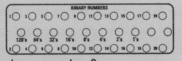

Before you start connecting the wires, place the binary numbers overlay in place over the LEDs. That's one of the pieces you punched out from the bottom of the workbench, remember?

Now connect the bare wire to 1-3-5-7-9-11-13-15-17-19. Then connect 19-49, 41-51-53.

To turn on a binary digit, connect a yellow wire onto spring 21. Test it out. Connect the battery, and touch the yellow wire to any one of the springs under the first eight LEDs.

So far, so good? Does that LED light? Great! We're in business (the binary business that is).

What's Going On?

Bits and bytes and binary are the basic building blocks of computers. Remember that computers can only count to two. But they do it many times and they do it very quickly. Computers use their own special number system called a "binary system." In binary, everything is either a zero or a one. Each one or zero is a bit, and 8 bits equals a byte. Computers use arrangements of up to eight bits (a byte) to represent letters and numbers.

Your binary overlay shows that each of the LEDs has been assigned a different number. Each of those numbers is the heading of a column like in our number system. Let's look at some numbers written in binary. Remember that when an LED is on it's a "1" and when it's off it's a "0."

Now Try This

In binary, 101 is the number 5. Let's build it! Connect 21-12-16. Connect the battery. This lights up the LEDs in the 1's and 4's column, creating 5.

4's	2's	1's
1	0	1

This is worth 1
This is worth 0
This is worth 4
5

To create the number 13 (which looks like 1101), disconnect the battery. Add a wire from spring 12 to spring 10 and reconnect the battery. You just added 8 to your 5, making the number 13. 5+8=13, I'd call that addition, wouldn't you?

8's	4's	2's	1's
1	1	0	1

This is worth 1
This is worth 0
This is worth 4
This is worth 8
13

How old are you?

35 in dog years, 101 in human binary years

Wanna try another one? 100110=38. Disconnect the battery and remove the wires from the LEDs. Connect 21-14-12-6 to make the number 38.

	32's	16's	8's	4's	2's	1's
38 =	1	0	0	1	1	0

Remove spring number 6 and you just subtracted 32. You've done the math problem 38 minus 32=? just like a computer would solve it.

Set up some of your own numbers and addition problems. Now you're beginning to think like a computer!

What numbers are these?
1001
100111
101110
1101101
11111111

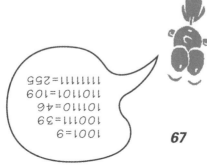

1001=9
100111=39
101110=46
1101101=109
11111111=255

67

Touch-Activated Light with Timer

This circuit uses aluminum foil wads to conduct electricity. Once it's hooked up, squeeze one wad of foil in each hand. The LED will light for a few seconds and then will go off.

Connect the bare wire to springs 1, 3, 5, 7, 9, 11, 13, 15, 17, and 19. Then hook up 19-40-61-59, 66-62-44-42, 60-53-51, 43-46-50-52, 45-49, 47-65, 2-48, yellow wire to 51, yellow wire to 39.

What's Going On?

Timing is everything! In this circuit you are making a touch timer. Squeeze and release the foil balls and you activate the timer. The LED will light for a few seconds and then go out. If it acts cranky, lick your fingers before touching the foil. (No, you won't get zapped. Really!)

The capacitor is the star of this circuit. It gets charged or filled up with electricity when you touch the foil. The LED stays on until the capaci-

drains. Touch the foil, the capacitor gets charged again and the whole thing happens all over again. The capacitor actually triggers a flip-flop switch to turn on. (Remember flip-flops from project #6?) When the capacitor drains, it triggers the flip-flop to turn off.

You've seen this timed light in some cars. You shut the door and the light stays on for a few seconds. (Hopefully it's long enough for you to collect your books, toys, jacket, and left-over lunch before leaving you in the dark.)

Some street lights and outdoor house lights are timed like this, too. They go on for a bit when someone trips the motion sensor. Only in this case, you just have to move in front of the sensor, you don't actually have to touch it.

Now Try This
What happens if you touch the two foil balls together? What about if you remove the foil and just touch the wires together?

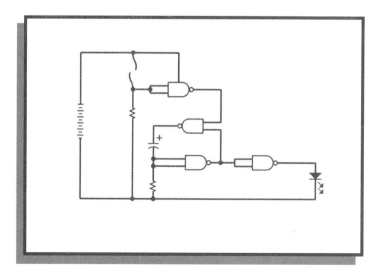

Lights from the Inside Out

> The LEDs from this circuit will start in the middle and spread out in both directions.
>
> Clear off the wires from your workbench and make sure the battery is disconnected.
>
> **Here are the connections: Connect the bare wire to springs 1, 3, 5, 7, 9, 11, 13, 15, 17, and 19. Then hook up 26-10, 24-8-12, 28-6-14, 34-4-16, 33-2-18, 22-37, 23-30, 27-36, 25-48-66, 42-44-57-65, 58-52-50-46, 19-40-38.**

I'm made up of lots of dots!

What's Going On?

This circuit shows the lights from the inside out. No, you don't take one of the LEDs apart. The sequence displays lights in the middle and then lights head out in both directions! Pretty cool, huh? Reader boards use this kind of light flashing to spell out words. But to you, the lights are flashing by so fast that they look like solid words or pictures. Flashing lights like these have been part of advertising since light bulbs have been part of our lives. But now that they can be digitized, they're everywhere! They can be made to change speed, and even to change patterns. The picture you see on a TV or a computer screen is a bunch of dots flashing. But they're flashing so fast they look like a solid picture.

Now Try This
You can double the pace by adding another resistor. First disconnect the battery, then add a wire from 57 to 55, and one from 58 to 56. Now reconnect the battery and watch your lights go double-time. Ha! And you thought resistors only slowed down electricity. Resistors are like a hose letting electricity through. When they're lined up in "series" (that's

electrical talk for being in a row), they slow down the flow. When they are in "parallel," it's like having two hoses instead of one, and you get twice as much electricity.

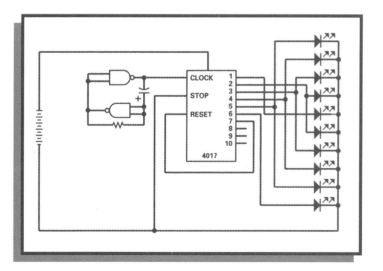

Congratulations! Give yourself a big hand, a pat on the back, a high five. You did it! You're a computer electronics pro, a technical wizard. This was no small feat.

By making all these projects you just took a lot of the mystery out of what's behind the monitor and what's beyond the keyboard. Computers have a big influence on our lives, but remember, it's people who run, program, and control the computers. With your newly acquired skills and knowledge of computer electronics, who knows what you'll do? This could be a kickoff to your career as a computer programmer, a webmaster, an electrical engineer, or a video game designer—the possibilities are endless!

To further your electronics skills, you may consider *Fun with Electronics*—a book and workbench much like this one. Instead of computer chips, Fun with Electronics has transistors, solar cells, diodes, and many other components used to create an engine sound, burglar alarm, radio, alarm clock, and much more! *Fun with Electronics* is available as a book and as a CD-ROM.

Your younger sister or brother may want to get into the electronics act with *Fun with Electronics, Jr.* With this book and kit, kids create their own circuit to power a fan, and make buzzers buzz and lights blink. It's electronics fun for the whole family.